One Last Cigarette

Lesiba Ignitiuas kekana

Published by Lesiba Ignitiuas kekana, 2022.

Table of Contents

One Last cigarette.

CHAPTER 1

Can I smoke a cigarette before I start with this book,Okay I'm done I feel dizzy and satisfied.My cigarette world started when I was 16. Most of my peers were smoking by that time, Yes it was cool too. By that time I was a non smoker I wasn't able to sit or be friends with anyone who smoke. I was those guy who was popular and wild , but smoking wasn't my thing. My mind started losing focus , usually I stay on my fit till the end of the journey but this time I got lost and trapped in my own thoughts. You know when you young you think everyone don't understand you. The reason I started smoking cigarette might be a little strange and different from yours but let me share.

It was Monday morning ,[phone ringing] I was asleep that time . My phone rang again. "who the hell is this calling at 4h30am In the morning . I picked up my phone, It was my mom " Tom wake up it's late, go bath and go to school." I snoozed for some couple of min, alright I took another 30 min nap. To be honest I don't know why I should wake so early in the morning when school starts at 08h30 but anywhere I got used to this routine. I will wait for my friend Ted at the gate so we can go to school together . "Dude you smoked cigarette?

you know I hate that, beside you going to get caught at school smelling like that, lets go to the nearest Indian shop Ted ! and buy some sweets for the smell " I know I grew up with Ted but the idea of him smoking I don't like it, I feel like I should just cut him off once and for all. I'm sorry I said that but sometimes there is good people in this world and there is bad people in this world I am a bad guy when coming to smoking. I was well discipline."Oh Gosh , is that the bell, dude we late let's go ! " " Tom you late again , sit down and take your report on your desk" said the teacher. " But ..Sir it's Monday how can I be.. " with anger ,the teacher Mr Jackson interrupted me " Sit down!! Arg maan!"

I took my report and sat . I opened my report

"REPORT

- ENGLISH fail
- Algebra fail
- Physics fail
- Trigonometry fail
- Chemistry fail

- Gym healthy pass
- Geography pass
- French fail
- Tourism pass

Term 1 : fail

"I felt like my heart pounding. What did I do wrong ? What went wrong? I study almost everyday . I lost confidence in myself. I slept the whole day on my desk luckily its was school holidays ,we were attending only for 3 hours at school. I quickly went home.

Classmate after class

After school

"Tom , Tom ! wait for me ." said Ted,10 fits behind me . " Can you hold this cigarette for me I want to show you some poster for some party we need to go .I don't really love the smell of cigarettes, it smoke it really somehow .

I held the cigarette " should I just smoke it, I got nothing to lose, It's whatever ". I took a pull . My skull was full of smoke I felt relieved from a moment and I started to cough so bad my eyes turned red" Ha-ha dude this is not for you bring my cigarette back" Ted said .

My 1st pull wasn't bad I thought I was going to be addicted to cigarettes from just smoking 1 cigarette . Afternoon I went to a supermarket " sir can you give me four cigarrete" I said " which one my boy, ain't you young for smoking young man" said the shopkeeper, " No Sir , It's for dad. Can I have that one with different flavours, Is it double switch,?" . "Are you sure your dad smoke double switch cigarette, ha-ha! Okay " shopkeeper laughed . He knew that it wasn't for my dad because most men here in my environment don't like smoking this double switch cigarette only women and young children, I didn't care , All I ever wanted is to forget about what just happened today at school. I started smoking one , I felt the excitement and the positivity in mind . It's hard for me to accept the fact that cigarette makes me feel free and happy but it really felt like a stress reliever , I smoked all four cigarette. I went back home to work on my school work . In the evening I got tired of studying I needed something that could take me out of miserable life right now . I took a walk in my neighbourhood , I went to nearest shop to buy a cigarette. While I was smoking I stared at people walking up and down , thinking about my goals in life, my failure in life and what I going to do in the future . I am a high school student I know this ain't no excuse for me to not get what but I want to be on top of the Great of all time. I was actually talking to the smoke that is full in my head . I enjoy this moment a lot so I decided to get myself another cigarette.

Part 2

I am basically a hypocrite to Ted . " Look at you , smelling like a cigarette, I can smell you from a distance ,ha-ha " he laughed . " ha-ha, you are really being dramatic. I bought some sweets dude what else you want from me." I said . " Dude I hate to say this but I feel like you are a hypocrite. Let me just leave it, we are all guys I understand . I think we should plan the party that's going to happen tonight " Ted said. What I know about tonight we going to get drunk perhaps I'll be more crazy than other days . Ted decided we should go for shopping , I always disagree with him but this time he got a point . I really need to look fresh and outstanding, this is the holiday I have to be on top of my peers . All I want is to be that guy people forever talks about , Good or bad it doesn't matter as long they are talking . Ted and I went shopping and I bought myself a pack of cigarette while he is busy buying alcohol for ourselves.We went outside the mall and sparked 2 cigarette. I saw 2 girls passing by , They looked confused about something , they also looked easy to approach and talks to maybe this is my chance to get someone. I approached them alone by the way while Ted is pretending to be on phone call . "Hello ladies , I'm Thomas , I saw this two alluring girls from a distance and came here . I would like to invite you two for a house party that is happening tonight , let me get your numbers so later if you two are free I can come over and pick you up" . One of them spoke " I hope the house party is fire ". I took my phone out and gave her to save her numbers .i smiled and said " You know mamacita I ain't going to invite you to a lame party , I hope,I see you guys later "they both are blushed and left. " Dude why you afraid of girls " I said on my way back to Ted while starring at him pretending to be on a phone call. " ha-ha to be honest those girls are hot but you know I need some drink to be on my moment, don't worry buddy tonight we going to get all hot girls " said Ted . " No brother, I took those girls numbers, we are sorted . Once we get there we do the most" I said.

At 16h00 we were ready . New clothes on , everything on point , before I put my shirt on I have to smoke cigarette. The only problem when I smoke cigarette I enjoy my moment for a long time and I end up smoking about 5 cigarettemaybe 7 perhaps. I went back inside ate, I put my shoes on, clothes and requested an uber . I called those girls that I met with this afternoon to send us their location . Yes they did, Ted and I like to make sure we never go wrong and we never look like a joke to our guest. We went to that party first . " Tom let's go drink first and I need to quickly use the bathroom and you'll find me inside I know you want to smoke some cigarette " said Ted . Ted is really a talkative person why doesn't he just get inside I'll find him inside without saying anything.Yes I did smoke that cigarette, while I was smoking I saw a girl that I wasn't suppose to see his name is I mean her name is Casey . This is the person I was trying to forget about long time ago and she saw me too . I knew she was going to come to me , she just one of those girls who have confidence and I don't really remember what was the cause of our broke up maybe because I moved on. " Thomas I see you still think you have it all." said Casey with a shocking face " Excuse me ugly girl, who are you? " . I saw how frustratedshe was , she wanted to make a scene luckily Ted out of no one he interrupted us . " Look here girl go stick with people who knows you " said Ted he grabbed my arm slowly and we went inside house with confidence since I was outside smoking . " Brother don't touch me like that " I said . " inside is fire okay call those girls and let go fetch them and

I'm sorry it's just that I wanted us to move away from that girl " then yes we went inside . It was really fire.

Part 3

I feel likeI could just leave here and go somewhere and be alone. I don't feel great here , I feel like there is something bothering me and I decided to go outside to smoke a cigarette . While I was smoking I was thinking " why do I feel somehow ? , is it normal ? And maybe it is. I'm becoming emotionally weak , I have to be a man and stay strong ". I need to go home , I went to Ted and tell him I'm not well I need to go . He insisted to accompany me home but

I said no I'll be fine . I went back home alone while I was smoking cigarettes. On my way home I smoked about 10 cigarrete.I was really stressed out suddenly on my way home through the house window while I was passing , I saw a drunk man hit his wife with a bottle on her head. I started to over think of how tough life is . I just looked away and walked home . I thinking deeply that everyone have problems in life, I have to gravitate with my problems until I beat them . I smoked another box of cigarrete before I reach home , so I can have an idea

of this steam and confusion in my head .

Finally I was home , I ate and took a nap . I

woke up in midnight , I wasn't fully awake

. My eyes were close but I could feel the

movement in my room . I wanted to wake

up but I couldn't , I was paralyzed. I could

feel something coming on my bed and I

heard a voice in my ear , a man's voice . "Do

you believe ? , Do you believe ? Do you

believe ? " said by a mysterious dark voice

. I was scared , I felt like it's over me and I

decided to open my eyes so I can see what it is . I saw a shadow and when I look up on my side of my bed I saw a whole from another world . I saw dinosaurs in it , I felt like I'm crazy . I prayed so hard , then it decided to leave me and I was able to move and wake up.

I felt like I'm really seeing species for the movies , Is this normal ? How can I explain this to someone? I calmed myself down and slept .

Part 4

A.Tips of how to stop smoking

Here are 10 ways/examples to help you resist the urge to smoke or use tobacco when a craving strikes.

1.Try nicotine replacement therapy

I prefer a therapy because this is the part where you learn why you smoke .This is also the part where you learn your weak point in life . Talking to yourself alone and analyzing your emotions and feelings to understand why you smoking is one of the keys .

1. Ask your health care provider about nicotine replacement therapy. The options include:

- Prescription nicotine in a nasal spray or inhaler
- Nicotine patches, gum and lozenges you can buy without a prescription
- Prescription non-nicotine stop-smoking drugs such as bupropion (Wellbutrin SR, Wellbutrin XL, others) and varenicline

Short-acting nicotine replacement therapies — such as nicotine gum, lozenges, nasal sprays or inhalers — can help you overcome intense cravings. These short-acting therapies are usually safe to use along with long-acting nicotine patches or one of the non-nicotine stop-smoking drugs.

Electronic cigarettes (e-cigarettes) have had a lot of interest recently as a replacement for smoking traditional cigarettes. But e-cigarettes haven't proved to be safer or more effective than nicotine-replacement medications in helping people stop smoking.

2. Avoid triggers

Tobacco urges are likely to be strongest in the places where you smoked or chewed tobacco most often, such as at parties or bars, or at times when you were feeling stressed or sipping coffee. Find out your triggers and have a plan in place to avoid them or get through them without using tobacco.

Don't set yourself up for a smoking relapse. If you usually smoked while you talked on the phone, for instance, keep a pen and paper nearby to keep busy with doodling rather than smoking.

3. Delay

If you feel like you're going to give in to your tobacco craving, tell yourself that you must first wait 10 more minutes. Then do something to distract yourself during that time. Try going to a public smoke-free zone. These simple tricks may be enough to move you past your tobacco craving.

4. Chew on it

Give your mouth something to do to resist a tobacco craving. Chew on sugarless gum or hard candy. Or munch on raw carrots, nuts or sunflower seeds — something crunchy and tasty.

5. Don't have 'just one'

You might be tempted to have just one cigarette to satisfy a tobacco craving. But don't fool yourself into thinking that you can stop there. More often than not, having just one leads to one more. And you may end up using tobacco again.

6. Get physical

Physical activity can help distract you from tobacco cravings. Even short bursts of activity — such as running up and down the stairs a few times — can make a tobacco craving go away. Get out for a walk or jog.

If you're at home or in the office, try squats, deep knee bends, pushups, running in place, or walking up and down a set of stairs. If you don't like physical activity, try prayer, sewing, woodwork or writing in a journal. Or do chores for distraction, such as cleaning or filing papers.

7. Try relaxation techniques

Smoking may have been your way to deal with stress. Fighting back against a tobacco craving can itself be stressful. Take the edge off stress by trying ways to relax, such as deep breathing, muscle relaxation, yoga, visualization, massage or listening to calming music.

8. Call for reinforcements

Connect with a family member, friend or support group member for help in your effort to resist a tobacco craving. Chat on the phone, go for a walk, share a few laughs, or meet to talk and support each other. Counseling can be helpful too.

9. Go online for support

Join an online stop-smoking program. Or read a quitter's blog and post encouraging thoughts for someone else who might be dealing with tobacco cravings. Learn from how others have handled their tobacco cravings.

10. Remind yourself of the benefits

Write down or say out loud why you want to stop smoking and resist tobacco cravings. These reasons might include:

- Feeling better
- Getting healthier
- Sparing your loved ones from secondhand smoke
- Saving money

Keep in mind that trying something to beat the urge to use tobacco is always better than doing nothing. And each time you resist a tobacco craving, you're one step closer to being tobacco-free.

Part 5

I decided to choose my own my methods to stop smoking , I was starting to be a heavy smoker by now . The method was to buy the last box of cigarette and try to save it as much as I can because that box was my last box of cigarettes that I will ever smoke . During the process my dad started to realize that I am smoking cigarettes, he asked me why then I told him the reasons . He told me that I mustn't worry too much about the things I see or dream about . His father (my grandfather) was a prophet perharps I might be one too , it runs in the family . What he will do is he'll take me to his fathers places he knows what he has to do .I was relieve in a way because I might be helped . After I had a talk with my dad, I went outside and smoked the 1st cigarette(19 cigarette left) .I'm planning to smoke to save all this cigarrete only and when they are finished it will be the last time I smoked . I start to see that I always smoke cigarettes in all occasions and even when I'm happy . I also did research above to help me stop smoking . I was also sick every single day , I could help myself but to sleep the whole day . I went outside but this time I took 3 cigarettes (16 cigarettes left) and went to India shop to smoke outside the shop . I smoked one cigarette while I was smoking , a saw a beautiful girl walking towards me . "Hey" she said . I greeted her back ,"can I please have one cigarette if you don't mind" she said that while blushing. I thought to myself that this girl is going to finish my cigarette.Then I gave her one cigarette, I smoked mine and she smoked the one I gave her. We talked and asked each other questions.she was free and she made me feel free too .I started to feel dizzy , she started to realizes that and after 2 min I collopsed.

I woke up , it was dark and I don't know this room . The girl I met at the Indian shop opened the door " Are you okay ?" I looked at her and I was surprised because I never seen a girl who ever cared about me especially a stranger . I responded yes I'm okay , I checked my pants pocket to see if the cigarettes still there . Luckly it was there , I went outside to smoke and she told me that her dad wasn't home I can be free to sleep over . I went outside with her and we smoked together the same cigarettes. She told me how she got into smoking and she want to quite . I told her my story and what I want to do to stop . She said she want to join me so we can walk this journey together .

She held my hand and told me that she thinks that I'm special and she want to express something new with me which is this journey . She got in my back and started to feel safe and loved . I felt like relationship is like a cigarette and everything in life is like a cigarette if you abuse it . I hope If we get to a toxic stage we can able to fix it and be strong enough to start all over again . School stresses me so much that's why I started to stop , I never failed a term in my life . This shows me if

I turn somewhere to erase my pain I'll eventually do it (in a different fields of life) I don't want to finish all the cigarettes I'm left with . At the same time my dad is telling me that I have a spiritual sickeness and he's planning to save money so we can go to mygrand father's places since is far it require a lot of money .

Her name was Lexie , I went home with Lexie the next day . I fetched that box of cigarettes and we went out to create more bond . I gave Lexie 4 cigarettes and I smoked 2 cigarettes (10 cigarettes left).Lexie started to tell me about her past , how abusive her life was . How her mother was abused by her father and how depressed she was . She said she that she wanted to smoke drugs and something just told him to not smoke it . It was really painful to hear everything from her past .

I took my last cigarette in that box and I gave Lexie the entire box (9 cigarettes left) she was surprised . I told her that we feed ourself with things to avoid our real problems . To be honest I want to be me if this world is going to mess my head up I better die mess up than a coward . I'll fight my failures, sickness and my addictions . I want to turn my suffering into good as I told Lexie . I know we all have problems and I'm not saying your problems are nothing to leave for but what I am saying is we have to stay strong . It's alright to feel like crying and emotions that's part of life .Lexie this is my last cigarette I will only smoke it if I have to , I'll challenge myself to the level that I never reached . It's better this way we are all human being , pain and problems. Will always place a role in our life .

Smoking helpline

Germany

German, English, French, Italian **0848 000 181**

The Helpline is available 11:00 to 19:00 Monday through Friday. Calls cost 8c/minute from landlines, more from mobiles. For counselling in Italian calls well be returned within 24 hours on weekdays.

Outside opening hours or in case all lines are busy, you can leave a message and the Quit Smoking Helpline will call you back. Call-backs are free of charge.

You can benefit from on-going counselling. The Quit Smoking Helpline will call you at agreed times and provide you with long-term counselling. Call-backs are free of charge.

United State of American

- Boys Town National Hotline[1]
    - 1 (800) 448-3000
    - Crisis and resource line staffed by counselors to provide information about a variety of issues, including drug dependency.

- Covenant House Teen Hotline (NineLine)[2]
    - 1 (800) 999-9999
    - General hotline for adolescents, teens and their families.

---

1. https://www.boystown.org/hotline/Pages/default.aspx

2. https://teenlineonline.org/yyp/covenant-house-nineline/

Assistance with any kind of problem—including alcohol and drug use. Covenant House specializes in homeless and runaway youth.

- National Council On Alcoholism And Drug Dependence, Inc. (NCADD)
  - 1 (800) NCA-CALL (622-2255)
  - NCADD's HOPE LINE directs callers to numerous affiliate programs around the country to assist, at a local level, with substance use issues.

- National Institute On Drug Abuse (NIDA)[3]
  - 1 (800) 662-HELP (4357)
  - National agency dedicated to prevention of drug use and treatment of existing drug problems. You can get around-the-clock help in finding local drug treatment centers.

- Substance Abuse And Mental Health Services Administration (SAMHSA) National Helpline[4]
  - 1 (800) 662-HELP (4357)
  - 1 (800) 487-4889 (TDD) for hearing impaired
  - Confidential information service for individuals and family members faced with substance use disorders and/or mental health issues. Information available in English and Spanish.

- National Suicide Prevention Lifeline[5]
  - 1 (800) 273-TALK (8255)
  - Not just a suicide hotline, this lifeline offers help with issues of drug and alcohol abuse.

- Partnership For Drug-Free Kids[6]

---

3. https://www.drugabuse.gov/

4. https://www.samhsa.gov/find-help/national-helpline

5. https://suicidepreventionlifeline.org/

6. https://drugfree.org/

- ○ 1 (855) DRUG-FREE (378-4373)
- ○ While not a crisis line, this hotline provides information to parents about adolescent and teen drug use, prevention and treatment.

You may be looking for local detox facilities and nearby rehab programs[7]. Many state government websites will also provide local drug and alcohol resources to those in need. To find your state government's website, do a web search for your state name and '.gov.' Once your state website is located, substance use resources shouldn't be hard to find and they should provide further phone contacts for your assistance. You can also contact American Addiction Centers[8] for free at (877) 947-4410

United Kingdom

England – Better health: Quit smoking[9]
<u>0300 123 1044</u> Lines are open 9am - 8pm weekdays, 11am -4pm at the weekend.

Scotland – Quit your way[10]
<u>0800 84 84 84</u> Lines are open 8am - 10pm weekdays, 9am-5pm at the weekend.

Wales – Help me quit[11]
<u>0800 085 2219</u> Lines are open Monday to Thursday, 8am -8pm, Friday 8am - 5pm and Saturday 9am - 4pm.

Northern Ireland – Want to Stop[12] For advice or to find your local stop-smoking service go to their website or text 'Quit' to 70004.

Child Abuse helpline

---

7.   https://drugabuse.com/addiction-treatment-centers/

8.   https://drugabuse.com/contact-us/

9.   https://www.nhs.uk/better-health/quit-smoking/

10.   https://www.nhsinform.scot/campaigns/quit-your-way-scotland

11.   https://www.helpmequit.wales/

12.   https://www.stopsmokingni.info/

Germany

Ludwigshafen, Germany
Website
http://www.saferinternet.de[13]

About the organisation

The German Safer Internet Centre (SIC DE) exists to promote a safer and better use of the internet and mobile technologies among children and young people.

Awareness centre

Description:klicksafe aims to promote people's online competence and to support them with a wide range of services to help them use the internet competently and critically. On the website, users can find a wealth of up-to-date information, practical tips and teaching material on digital services and topics. The target groups are teachers, educators, parents, children, young people and multipliers.

klicksafe is politically and economically independent and is implemented by the Media Authority of Rhineland-Palatinate (coordinator) and the State Media Authority of North Rhine-Westphalia.

The key platform www.klicksafe.de[14] offers access to the whole portfolio of materials.

Email address: info@klicksafe.de
Website: http://www.klicksafe.de[15]
Social media:
https://www.facebook.com/klicksafe
https://twitter.com/klicksafe
https://www.youtube.com/user/klicksafegermanyhttps://www.instagram.com/klicksafe

Helpline

Description:
Nummer gegen Kummer e.V. (NgK) is the umbrella organisation of the largest toll-free and anonymous counselling service for children, adolescents, parents and other carers in Germany and looks back on 40 years of experience as a general helpline.

Since 2008, NgK is the national helpline within the German Safer Internet Centre (SIC). Young people can call the Child helpline at 116111 (peer-to-peer counselling on Saturdays) or contact the online counselling services (chat, e-mail) via the website

---

13.   http://www.saferinternet.de/

14.   http://www.klicksafe.de/

15.   http://www.klicksafe.de/

www.nummergegenkummer.de[16]. The parent's helpline can be reached via 0800 – 111 0 550.

The helpline is open to all topics, including online safety issues, and offers a safe place to talk, seek advice, comfort or simply a sympathetic ear. NgK's trained volunteer counsellors support those seeking advice to find their own solutions (by helping them to help themselves). If needed, counsellors can provide information about specialised/professional help or recommend relevant (online) sources of information enabling young people or parents to further educate themselves.

Email address: info@nummergegenkummer.de

Website: https://www.nummergegenkummer.de[17]

Social media:

https://www.facebook.com/ngk.dachverband

https://www.youtube.com/c/NummergegenKummereVhttps://www.instagram.com/nummergegenkummer_e.v

Hotline

Description:

The German Safer Internet Centre (SIC) has two national alert platforms for reporting of illegal content on the internet, particularly in respect of child pornography, racism and xenophobia: IBSDE[18], operated by the hotlines of eco and FSM as independent partners, and jugendschutz.net[19].

As a consortium set up by the partners eco and FSM, IBSDE is 'industry driven' and has a self-regulatory approach. eco is the Internet Service Providers Association in Germany and represents organisations of the (German) internet industry, as well as all enterprises that make commercial use of the internet. FSM is the German non-profit association for voluntary self-regulation in online and mobile media and was founded by numerous media associations and media enterprises. Its members are media and telecommunications organisations, as well as companies who offer their products and services online.

jugendschutz.net is a government institution and was established as an initiative of the Youth Ministers of the German Federal States. As a competence centre for the protection of minors on the internet, jugendschutz.net looks closely at risks in services specifically attractive to young users. Risky contacts, self-harm behaviour, political extremism and the sexual exploitation of children is the focus of jugendschutz.net's work.

---

16.   https://www.nummergegenkummer.de/

17.   https://www.nummergegenkummer.de/

18.   https://www.internet-beschwerdestelle.de/

19.   https://jugendschutz.net/

The hotline partners are collaborating closely, for example by regular meetings, exchange of expertise and participation in joint projects.

The hotline website addresses are:

www.fsm.de/de[20]

www.eco.de[21]

beschwerdestelle.eco.de[22]

www.jugendschutz.net[23]

www.internet-beschwerdestelle.de[24]

The hotline email addresses are:

office@fsm.de

hotline@eco.de

buero@jugendschutz.net

Social media:

https://www.facebook.com/fsm.de/

https://twitter.com/FSM_de

https://www.youtube.com/user/FSMBerlinhttps://twitter.com/eco_politik

Youth participation

Description:

The klicksafe Youth Panel consists of a group of students concerned with digital trends and relevant issues of the online world. As media scouts, they help younger students navigate through the digital universe via talks on Facebook, WhatsApp and more. Since January 2009, klicksafe has coordinated a cooperative Youth Panel with representatives from different secondary schools.

Information on the Youth Panel is available on the klicksafe website[25].

Email address: rack@medienanstalt-rlp.de

United state of American

If you would like more information on child abuse, need assistance reporting abuse, or to speak with a Childhelp counselor, please call or text the Childhelp National Child Abuse Hotline at **1-800-4-A-CHILD (1-800-422-4453). You can also live chat with**

---

20.   http://www.fsm.de/de

21.   https://www.eco.de/

22.   http://beschwerdestelle.eco.de/

23.   http://www.jugendschutz.net/

24.   http://www.internet-beschwerdestelle.de/

25.   https://www.klicksafe.de/ueber-klicksafe/die-initiative/project-information-en/youth-und-childrens-panel-english/youth-panel-introduction/

a trained counselor at **www.childhelphotline.org**[26]. The hotline is available 24 hours a day and all calls are confidential. For more information on the hotline, visit www.childhelp.org/hotline[27].

If you are contacting Childhelp to receive assistance in reporting abuse, **please do not use the email option below**. Please call or text the Childhelp National Child Abuse Hotline at **1-800-4-A-CHILD (1-800-422-4453)**. **You can also live chat with a trained counselor at www.childhelphotline.org**[28]. While the hotline is available 24 hours a day, email inquiries have a 24-48 hour response time (Monday-Friday). Additionally, emails are not confidential.

For media inquiries and communications, please email Daphne Young at dyoung@childhelp.org or contact her by phone at (480) 922-8212 ext. 446.

For recurring gift inquiries please contact gifts@childhelp.org.

Canada

Childhelp National Child Abuse Hotline[29]
1-800-4ACHILD or 1-800-422-4453 | TDD: 1-800-2A-CHILD. 24/7 - Call from: USA, Canada, Puerto Rico, Guam or the Virgin Islands. - can help in 170 languages. All calls are confidential.
Operation Come Home[30]
Toll-Free 1 800 668 4663 | Local 613 230 4663 - 8am-4pm Monday to Friday.

Swiss

SWAGAA[31] - + 268 505 7514

South Africa

---

26.   **http://www.childhelphotline.org/**

27.   https://www.childhelp.org/hotline/

28.   **http://www.childhelphotline.org/**

29.   http://www.childhelp.org/get_help

30.   http://operationcomehome.ca/programs/reunite/

31.   https://www.facebook.com/Swaziland-Action-Group-Against-Abuse-SWAGAA-
202248446510926/

Childline SouthAfrica[32] - 0800 055 555

<u>Women abuse helpline</u>

<u>Germany</u>

1. National Emergency Hotline: 911. Aleng Pulis Hotline: 0919 777 7377. ...

<u>United state of American</u>

The Office on Violence Against Women reduces violence against women. They help victims of domestic violence, dating violence, sexual assault, and stalking.

Acronym:

OVW

Website:

<u>Office on Violence Against Women</u>[33]

Contact:

<u>Contact the Office on Violence Against Women</u>[34]

Local Offices:

<u>Find help near you</u>[35]

Main Address:

U.S. Department of Justice
Office on Violence Against Women

---

32.   http://www.childlinesa.org.za/

33. https://www.justice.gov/ovw

34. https://www.justice.gov/ovw/contact-ovw

35. https://www.justice.gov/ovw/local-resources

145 N Street, NE, Suite 10W.121
Washington, DC 20530

Email:

ovw.info@usdoj.gov

Phone Number:

1-202-307-6026

Toll Free:

1-800-799-7233 (Domestic Violence Hotline)
1-800-656-4673 (Sexual Assault Hotline)
1-866-331-9474 (Teen Dating Abuse Helpline)
1-855-484-2846 (Victim Hotline)

TTY:

1-202-307-2277
1-800-787-3224 (Domestic Violence Hotline)
1-866-331-8453 (Teen Dating Abuse Helpline)

Australia

IF YOU ARE AT RISK

If you, or someone you know, is in immediate danger, call 000.

NATIONAL

1800RESPECT

(1800 737 732)

The National Sexual Assault, Family & Domestic Violence Counselling Line for any Australian who has experienced, or is at risk of, family and domestic violence and/or sexual assault.

24 hours, 7 days a week.

www.1800respect.org.au[36]

36.　　https://www.1800respect.org.au/

Lifeline

(13 11 14)

A national number which can help put you in contact with a crisis service in your state.

24 hours, 7 days a week.

www.lifeline.org.au[37]

AUSTRALIAN CAPITAL TERRITORY

Domestic Violence Crisis Service (DVCS)

(02 6280 0900)

Crisis intervention and counselling, family violence intervention program, education and information for the community.

24 hours, 7 days a week.

www.dvcs.org.au[38]

Canberra Rape Crisis Centre (CRCC)

(02 6247 2525)

Crisis support, counselling advocacy and support programs for men and women.

7am -10.30pm

On call for ACT Health and Police

www.crcc.org.au[39]

NEW SOUTH WALES

NSW Domestic Violence Line

(1800 656 463 / TTY 1800 671 442)

Provides telephone counselling, information and referrals for women and same-sex partners who are experiencing or have experienced domestic violence.

24 hours, 7 days a week.

www.community.nsw.gov.au[40]

NSW Rape Crisis

(1800 424 017)

Provides telephone and online counselling for anyone who is or has experienced sexual violence and their supporters,

24 hours, 7 days a week.

www.rape-dvservices.org.au[41]

NORTHERN TERRITORY

---

37.   https://www.lifeline.org.au/

38.   https://dvcs.org.au/

39.   http://www.crcc.org.au/

40.   https://www.facs.nsw.gov.au/families

41.   https://www.rape-dvservices.org.au/

Catherine Booth House
(8981 5928)

Short term crisis accommodation, referral and support for adult and young women over 18 years old.

24 hours, 7 days a week.

www.shelterme.org.au[42]

Darwin Aboriginal and Islander Women's Shelter (DAIWS)
(08 8945 2284)

Support, referral, outreach and domestic violence crisis accomodation for Aboriginal and Torres Strait Islander women who are homeless or escaping family violence.

24 hours, 7 days a week.

Dawn House (Darwin)
(08 8945 1388)

Crisis accomodation and support service for women with children who are experiencing or escaping domestic or family violence.

24 hours, 7 days a week.

www.dawnhouse.org.au[43]

Ruby Gaea (Darwin)
(08 8945 0155)

Free counselling and support to women and children who have experience sexual assault at any time in their life.

Monday – Friday 8.30am to 5pm.

www.rubygaea.net.au[44]

Sexual Assault Referral Centre (Darwin)
(08 8922 6472)

Free 24-hour emergency service that provids crisis counselling and other support needs to both adult and children who have experienced any form of sexual assault or sexual abuse, either recently or in the past.

24 hours, 7 days a week.

www.health.nt.gov.au/sexual_assault_services[45]

Sexual Assault Referral Centre (Alice Springs)
(08 8955 4500)

Free 24-hour emergency service that provids crisis counselling and other support needs to both adult and children who have experienced any form of sexual assault or sexual abuse, either recently or in the past.

42.	https://www.shelterme.org.au/

43.	https://www.dawnhouse.org.au/

44.	http://www.rubygaea.net.au/

45.	https://nt.gov.au/wellbeing/hospitals-health-services/sexual-assault-referral-centres

24 hours, 7 days a week.

www.health.nt.gov.au/sexual_assault_services[46]

QUEENSLAND

DVConnect Womensline

(1800 811 811)

Free state wide telephone service that provides confidential counselling and referral to crisis accommodation for women and children affected by domestic or family Violence and those who are concerned about a friend or family member.

24 hours, 7 days a week.

www.dvconnect.org/womensline[47]

DVConnect Mensline

(1800 600 636)

Free state wide telephone service that provides counselling and referral for men for a range of issues especially those who have experienced or use domestic and family violence and those who are concerned about a friend or family member.

9am – 12 midnight, 7 days a week.

www.dvconnect.org/mensline[48]

DVConnect Sexual Assault Helpline

(1800 010 120)

Telephone service that provides counselling to women, men and young people who have experienced or are concerned someone they know has experienced sexual assault or abuse.

7.30am – 11.30pm, 7 days a week.

dvconnect.org/queensland-sexual-assault-helpline/[49]

SOUTH AUSTRALIA

Domestic Violence and Aboriginal Family Violence Gateway Services

(1800 800 098)

Counselling and support for women experiencing domestic and family violence.
24 hours, 7 days a week.

womenssafetyservices.com.au[50]

Yarrow Place Rape and Sexual Assault Services

(1800 817 421)

---

46.   https://nt.gov.au/wellbeing/hospitals-health-services/sexual-assault-referral-centres

47.   http://www.dvconnect.org/womensline/

48.   http://www.dvconnect.org/mensline/

49.   http://www.dvconnect.org/queensland-sexual-assault-helpline/

50.   http://womenssafetyservices.com.au/

(After hours and emergency 08 8226 8787)

Lead public health agency responding to adult rape and sexual assault in South Australia for people aged 16 years and over.

24 hours, 7 days a week.

www.sahealth.sa.gov.au[51]

TASMANIA

Safe at Home Family Violence Response and Referral Line (1800 633 937)

Tasmanian information and referral service where callers are able to access the full range of response, counselling, information and other support services provided by Safe at Home.

24 hours, 7 days a week.

www.safeathome.tas.gov.au[52]

Family Violence Counselling and Support Service (1800 608 122)

Family Violence Counselling and Support Service offers professional and specialised services to assist children, young people and adults affected by family violence.

9am to midnights weekdays and 4pm to midnight weekends and public holidays.

www.dhhs.tas.gov.au[53]

VICTORIA

Safe Steps Family Violence Response Centre (1800 015 188)

Victorian statewide service providing telephone support, information, referral, safety planning and risk assessment for women and children experiencing family violence.

24 hours, 7 days a week.

www.safesteps.org.au[54]

Sexual Assault Crisis Line (1800 806 292)

A statewide confidential, telephone crisis counselling service for people who have experienced both past and recent sexual assault.

24 hours, 7 days a week.

www.sacl.com.au[55]

WESTERN AUSTRALIA

51.	https://www.sahealth.sa.gov.au/wps/wcm/connect/Public+Content/SA+Health+Internet/Services/

Primary+and+Specialised+Services/Sexual+Health+Services/Yarrow+Place/Yarrow+Place

52.	https://www.safeathome.tas.gov.au/

53.	https://www.dhhs.tas.gov.au/

54.	https://www.safesteps.org.au/

55.	http://www.sacl.com.au/

Women's Domestic Violence Helpline (1800 007 339)

Statewide service providing support and counselling for women experiencing family and domestic violence.

24 hours, 7 days a week.

Sexual Assault Resource Centre
1800 199 888

Statewide service providing emergency services and counselling for people who have experienced both past and recent sexual assault.

https://www.kemh.health.wa.gov.au/Our-services/Statewide-Services/SARC

Canada

Ontario

Assaulted Women's Helpline: Provides anonymous and confidential crisis counseling, informational and emotional support to women. (Toronto, ON)

http://www.awhl.org/

Toll Free: 1-866-863-0511

Toll Free TTY: 1-866-863-7868

Talk for Healing: Talk4Healing is a helpline available to all Aboriginal women living in urban, rural and remote communities, both on and off reserve, throughout Northern Ontario.

http://www.talk4healing.com/

Telephone: 1-855-554-4325

Mental Health Crisis Line: A 24/7 helpline to assist people experiencing a mental health problem or crisis. (Ottawa, ON)

http://www.crisisline.ca/home.htm

Telephone: 613-722-6914

Toll Free: 1-866-996-0991

Fem'aide: Provincial helpline for francophone women in Ontario dealing with violence

http://www.femaide.ca/

Telephone: 1-877-336-2433

TTY: 1-866-860-7082

British Columbia

Battered Women's Support Services: Provides education, advocacy and support services to assist women. (Vancouver, BC)

http://www.bwss.org/

Crisis line: 604-687-1867

Toll Free: 1-855-687-1868

Greater Vancouver Crisis Line: Non-profit organizing that provides emotional support to youth, adults and seniors in distress. (Greater Vancouver, BC)

Telephone: 604-872-3311

Toll Free: 1-866-661-3311

TTY: 1-866-872-0113

Domestic Violence Helpline (Victim Link): Helpline designed to provide information and support to those experiencing domestic violence.

http://www.domesticviolencebc.ca/

Phone: 604-875-0885

Toll Free TTY: 1-800-563-0808

Surrey Women's Center: Offer a range of crisis services to victims of domestic violence, sexual assault, child abuse and other forms of family violence. 24/7 helpline services provided. (Surrey, BC)

http://surreywomenscentre.ca/

Telephone: 604-583-1295

WAVAW: Works to end violence against women through various support programs and services including an emotional and informational support 24-hour crisis line.

http://www.wavaw.ca/

24-Hour Crisis Line: 604-255-6344

Toll free: 1-877-392-7583

North Shore Crisis Services Society: NSCSS is a transition house and also provides related support services. (North Vancouver, BC)

http://nscss.net/

Telephone: 604-987-3374

BC Coalition to Eliminate Abuse of Seniors: Helpline providing emotional and legal information and referral for seniors experiencing abuse. (Vancouver, BC)

http://bcceas.ca/

Telephone: 604-437-1940

Toll free: 1-866-437-1940

TTY: 604-428-3359

TTY Toll free: 1-855-306-1443

Alberta

Crisis Association of Vegreville: General helpline for those experiencing a problem and require assistance. (Vegreville, Alberta)

Telephone: 1-780-632-2233

Toll Free Helpline: 1-780-632-7070

Family Violence Info Line: 24/7 helpline in over 170 languages to provide support and advice for people experiencing family violence.

Telephone: 780- 310-1818

Edmonton Women's Shelter Ltd.: A non-profit agency with three shelters for women with or without children leaving domestic violence situations. A 24 hour support and information line is provided. (Edmonton, AB)

http://www.winhouse.org/

Telephone: 780-479-0058

St. Paul's Crisis Center: Non-profit organization that provides safe and supportive environments for women with or without children who are experiencing family violence. 24/7 crisis line available for information and emotional support. (St. Paul, AB)

http://www.stpaulcrisiscentre.ca/

Telephone: 645-5195

Toll Free: 1-800-263-3045

Camrose Women's Shelter Society: Women's shelter proving safe environments for women and children needing protection from family violence. 24 hour crisis line for additional assistance. (Camrose, AB)

http://brigantiaplace.org/

Phone: 780-672-1035 (main line)

Toll Free Crisis Line: 1-877-672-1010

Calgary Women's Emergency Shelter: Offers support to individuals and families fleeing family violence and abuse. The 24-hour helpline provides support, information and access to programs at the shelter. (Calgary, AB)

http://www.calgarywomensshelter.com/home

Telephone: 403-234-7233

Toll Free: 1 (866) 606-7233

Sucker Creek Women's Emergency Shelter: Provides range of services for women and children experiencing abuse and assault including a 24-hour crisis line.(Edmonton, AB)

Telephone: 780-523-2929

Crisis Phone: 780-523-4357

Toll Free: 1-866-523-2929

Saskatchewan

La Ronge 24-Hour Crisis Line: General crisis line for men and women in crisis in La Ronge, Saskatchewan. (La Ronge, SK)

Crisis Line: 306-425-4090

Moose Jaw Domestic Violence Crisis Line: Moose Jaw offers a transition house for women and children affected by family violence and abuse. The crisis line offers 24-hour emotional, informational and referral support to women. (Moose Jaw, SK)

http://www.mj-transitionhouse.com/

Hotline: 306-693-6511

Prince Albert Domestic Violence Crisis Intervention: General crisis line for those experiencing domestic violence. (Prince Albert, SK)

Crisis Line: 306-764-1011

Yorkton Domestic Violence Crisis Line: General crisis line for those experiencing domestic violence in Yorkton. (Yorkton, SK)

Crisis Line: 1-888-783-3111

(Regina) Crisis/Suicide Line: Provides 24-hour social and health crisis response to community of Regina. (Regina, SK)

http://www.mobilecrisis.ca/

Telephone: 306-757-0127

Crisis Line: 306-525-5333

Manitoba

Toll-Free Province Wide Domestic Abuse Crisis Line (24 hours): General crisis line for people experiencing domestic violence and abuse in the province of Manitoba.

Toll Free: 1-877-977-0007

Klinic Crisis Line: Offers confidential counseling, support and referral to people in crisis.
http://www.klinic.mb.ca/
Crisis Line: (204) 786-8686
Toll free: 1-888-322-3019
TTY (204) 784-4097
Northwest Territories
NWT Help Line: General helpline there to provide support to those in crisis.
Telephone: 1-800-661-0844
Nunavut
Nunavut Kamatsiaqtut Help Line: Provides anonymous and confidential counseling for northerners in crisis.
http://www.nunavuthelpline.ca/
Telephone: 867-979-3333
Toll Free: 1-800-265-3333
Quebec
Domestic Violence Hotline: Provides anonymous and confidential domestic violence services via telephone or email. (Montreal, QC)
www.sosviolenceconjugale.ca
Telephone: 514-873-9010
Toll free: 1-800-363-9010
Newfoundland
Hope Haven Transition House Crisis Line: Provides confidential and safe emergency shelter to women and children who are experiencing violence and abuse. 24-hour crisis line offers information, emergency planning and emotional support. (Labrador City, NL)
http://www.hopehaven.ca/
Crisis Line: (709) 944-6900
Toll Free: 1-888-332-0000
Nova Scotia
Helpline: General helpline for people experiencing crisis in Nova Scotia.
Toll Free: 1-877-521-1188
TTY: 1-855-443-2660
Yukon
Kaushee's Place / Yukon Women's Transition Home: Offers shelter, outreach, support and advocacy for women and their children fleeing abuse.
http://www.womensdirectorate.gov.yk.ca/shelters.html
Crisis Line: 867-668-5733 (collect calls accepted from outside Whitehorse)
Telephone: 867-633-7720

Swiss

For persons affected by violence

In an emergency

Police: www.polizei.ch, tel. 117
Medical assistance: www.erstehilfe.ch, tel. 144

Information on and addresses of free, confidential and anonymous advice units throughout Switzerland

www.opferhilfe-schweiz.ch

Addresses of shelters

https://opferhilfe-schweiz.ch/de/was-ist-opferhilfe/schutz/
www.frauenhaus-schweiz.ch

For perpetrators of violence

Addresses for advice and training programmes:
www.fvgs.ch

Address for enquiries

Federal Office for Gender Equality
Schwarztorstrasse 51
3003 Bern

Publisher

Federal Office for Gender Equality
https://www.ebg.admin.ch/ebg/en/home.html [56]
General Secretariat FDHA
http://www.edi.admin.ch [57]

South African

---

56.   https://www.ebg.admin.ch/ebg/en/home.html

57.   http://www.edi.admin.ch/

Women Abuse – Call: ? <u>**0800 150 150**</u>

<u>Depression/suicidal helplines</u>

<u>Germany</u>

+49 176 62371658[58]

Gotenstraße 74, 10829 Berlin, Germany[59]

<u>United States of America</u>

The **National Suicide Prevention Lifeline** is a United States-based suicide prevention[60]network of over 160 crisis centers that provides 24/ 7 service[61] via a toll-free hotline with the number **1 (800) 273-8255** (**TALK**). It is available to anyone in suicidal crisis or emotional distress

<u>Australian</u>

---

58.   https://www.google.co.za/

search?q=germany+mental+health+services&client=safari&hl=en-

za&sxsrf=ALiCzsbxql9UBb4y9hizPNw08PGGHDf8Mw%3A1653960985469&ei=GXGVYqW

iHJiO8gLtqICQBQ&oq=germany+depression%2Fsuicide+helpline+for+german+citizens&gs_l

cp=ChNtb2JpbGUtZ3dzLXdpei1zZXJwEAEYATIHCCMQsAMQJzIHCAAQRxCwAzIHCA

AQRxCwAzIHCAAQRxCwAzIHCAAQRxCwAzIHCAAQRxCwAzIHCAAQRxCwAzIHC

AAQRxCwAzIHCAAQRxCwA0oECEEYAFAAWABg-

jVoAXAAeACAAQCIAQCSAQCYAQDIAQnAAQE&sclient=mobile-gws-wiz-serp

59.   https://www.google.co.za/

search?q=germany+mental+health+services&client=safari&hl=en-

za&sxsrf=ALiCzsbxql9UBb4y9hizPNw08PGGHDf8Mw%3A1653960985469&ei=GXGVYqW

iHJiO8gLtqICQBQ&oq=germany+depression%2Fsuicide+helpline+for+german+citizens&gs_l

cp=ChNtb2JpbGUtZ3dzLXdpei1zZXJwEAEYATIHCCMQsAMQJzIHCAAQRxCwAzIHCA

AQRxCwAzIHCAAQRxCwAzIHCAAQRxCwAzIHCAAQRxCwAzIHCAAQRxCwAzIHC

AAQRxCwAzIHCAAQRxCwA0oECEEYAFAAWABg-

jVoAXAAeACAAQCIAQCSAQCYAQDIAQnAAQE&sclient=mobile-gws-wiz-serp

60.   https://en.m.wikipedia.org/wiki/Suicide_prevention

61.   https://en.m.wikipedia.org/wiki/24/7_service

Every 30 seconds, a person in Australia reaches out to Lifeline for help.

We are a national charity providing all Australians experiencing emotional distress with access to 24 hour crisis support and suicide prevention services.

Call 13 11 14

Canada

https://www.crisisservicescanada.ca/call-us/

South Africa

Call :0800567567

Swiss

https://www.143.ch/

Drug abusing counseling contact (Germany)

Altona

KDROBS Altona, Hohenesch 13-17, 22765 Hamburg, Phone: 040/3908640/ -41, Email: altona@kodrobs.de, Mon, Tue & Thu: 10 a.m. - 7 p.m., ENG

Kajal Frauenperspektiven, Substance abuse counselling for women, Haubachstraße 78, 22767 Hamburg, Phone: 040/ 3806987, Email: kajal@frauenperspektiven.de, Mon, Wed, Thu & Fri: 9 a.m. - 5 p.m., Tue: 2:30 p.m. - 5 p.m. Sat: 12 p.m. - 5 p.m., ENG & FR

Lukas Suchthilfezentrum, Luruper Hauptstr. 138, 22547 Hamburg, Phone: 040/ 970770, Mon & Thu: 9 a.m. - 6 p.m., Tue & Wed: 10 a.m. - 6 p.m., Fri: 10 a.m. - 3 p.m., ENG

Palette Bartelsstraße 12, 20357 Hamburg, Phone: 040/ 4302590, Email: bartesstrasse@palette-hamburg.de, Mon - Fri: 11 a.m. - 4 p.m., ENG, FA

Bergedorf

KODROBS Bergedorf, Lohbrügger Landstraße 6, 21031 Hamburg, Phone: 040/ 72160-38/ -39, Email: bergedorf@kodrobs.de, Mon, Tue & Fri: 10 a.m. - 5 p.m., Thu: 10 a.m. - 7 p.m.,ENG, RU, ES

Eimsbüttel

UKE University Hospital, Drug and alcohol walk-in clinic, Martinistraße 52, 20246 Hamburg, Phone: 040/ 741054217, Email: drogenambulanz@uke.de, open 24/7, Interpreters for most languages can be arranged.

Frauenperspektiven Substance abuse counselling for women, Charlottenstraße 26, 20257 Hamburg, Phone: 040/ 4329600, Email: beratungsstelle@frauenperspektiven.de, Mon, Wed & Thu: 10 a.m. - 4 p.m., Fri: 10 a.m. - 2 p.m., ENG

M.A.T. West, Elbgaustraße 83, 22523 Hamburg, Phone: 040/ 57193131, Email: mat-west@therapiehilfe.de, ENG, FA

Hamburg Mitte (Centre)

Büro für Suchtprävention, Repsoldstraße 4, 20097 Hamburg, Phone: 040/ 2849918-24, Email: hls@sucht-hamburg.de, Interpreters for most languages can be arranged.

Drob Inn St. Georg Directed specifically at opiate users, Besenbinderhof 71, 20097 Hamburg, Phone: 040/ 3999930, Email: drob.inn@jugendhilfe.de, Mon, Wed, Thu & Fri: 9 a.m. - 5 p.m., Tue: 2:30 p.m. - 5 p.m., Sat: 12 p.m. - 5 p.m.

KODROBS Wilhelmsburg, Weimarer Straße 83-85, 21107 Hamburg,   Phone: 040/   7216038/   -39,   Email:

wilhelmsburg@kodrobs.de, Mon, Tue & Thu: 10 a.m. - 7 p.m., Fri: 10 a.m. - 4 p.m., ENG, RU, KU, TR

Viva Billstedt - Take Care! Substance abuse counselling for young adults, Ruhmkoppel 14, 22119, Phone: 040/ 707020020 or 0151/ 59278822, Email: takecare-billstedt@jugendhilfe.de, open upon request, ENG

Hamburg Nord (North)

MobS Hamburg Nord Substance abuse counselling for young adults, Wischhöfen 1, 22415 Hamburg, Phone: 040/ 55440753, Email: mobs-nord@therapiehilfe.de, open upon request, ENG, RU, POL, FA

Harburg

OkayM.A.T. & Seehaus Harburg, Schlossmühlendamm 8-10, 21073 Hamburg, Phone: 040/ 7679490, Email: mat-harburg@therapiehilfe.de, Mon & Thu: 2 p.m. - 4 p.m., ENG, FA

STZ Harburg, Knoopstraße 37, 21073 Hamburg, Phone: 040/ 3347533-0, Email: lars.ehricke@martha-stiftung.de, Mon, Wed & Thu: 10 a.m. - 6 p.m., Tue: 2 p.m. - 6 p.m., Fri: 10 a.m. - 3 p.m., ENG, ESP

MobS Therapiehilfe, Cuxhavener Straße 386, 21149 Hamburg, Phone: 040/ 30384444, Email: mobs-harburg@therapiehilfe.de, open upon request, **ENG, POL, RU**

Wandsbek

Die Boje Suchthilfe, Brauhausstieg 15-17, 22041 Hamburg, Phone: 040/ 444091 or 040/ 7314949, Email: beratung@dieboje.de, Mon - Fri: 10 a.m. - 6 p.m., **ENG**

Die Brücke Eilbek, Conventstraße 14, 22089 Hamburg, Phone: 040/ 6683638, Tue: 3 p.m. - 5 p.m., **ENG**

Die Brücke Wandsbek, Walddörferstraße 337, 22047 Hamburg, Phone: 040/ 6683637, Email: info@ambulante-suchttherapie.de, Tue: 5 p.m. - 7 p.m., Thu: 3 p.m. - 5 p.m., **ENG, ESP**

Viva Wandsbek - Take Care! Substance abuse counselling for young adults, Bei den Höfen 23, 22043 Hamburg, Phone: 040/ 244242590 or

0177/ 2094549, Email: takecare@jugendhilfe.de, Mon - Wed: 10 a.m. - 6 p.m., Thu & Fri: 1 p.m. 6 p.m., **ENG**

Therapeutische Gemeinschaft Jenfeld (TGJ), Jenfelder Straße 100, 22045 Hamburg, Phone: 040/ 65409628, Email: info.aha@alida.de, Mon & Thu: 3 p.m. - 5 p.m., **ENG**

Australia

The phone service is available 24/ by calling (08) **9442 5000** or **1800 198 024** (toll-free for country callers).

Live Chat is also free of charge and available for Western Australian residents Monday to Friday 7.30am - 9pm, Saturday 9am - 7pm and Sunday 11am - 6pm. Live Chat can be accessed here[62].

Email: alcoholdrugsupport@mhc.wa.gov.au

Web: alcoholdrugsupport.mhc.wa.gov.au[63]

South African

Elim Clinic (Drug Abuse Treatment Centre)

– **Call:** 011 975 2951 (**Get Hours**)

– **Website:** www.elimclin.co.za[64]

United States of America

DrugAbuse.com[65] hotline: Addiction Navigators on call 24/ 7 to help answer any questions related to drug abuse and support

- Al-Anon[66] and Ala-teen[67] hotline line: 800-356-9996

---

62.   https://www.mhc.wa.gov.au/about-us/our-services/alcohol-and-drug-support-service/live-chat-with-an-alcoholdrug-counsellor/

63.   http://alcoholdrugsupport.mhc.wa.gov.au/

64.   http://www.elimclin.co.za/

65. https://drugabuse.com/addiction/drug-abuse/hotlines/

66. https://al-anon.org/

– Counselors provide support to teens and adults who are negatively impacted by alcohol addiction and provide resources to group therapy nearby for ongoing support.

- Substance Abuse and Mental Health Services Administration[68] (SAMHSA): 1-800-662-4357 – English/Spanish speaking counselors provide referrals to treatment facilities, support groups, and community-based services.
- National Suicide Prevention[69]: 1-800-273-8255 – Support to help those in crisis process their emotional distress and prevent suicide.
- Boys Town[70]: 1-800-448-3000 – Over 140 languages can be translated; they also provide a telecommunications device for the deaf (TDD) line for the speech and hearing impaired (1-800-448-1833).
- Drugfree.org[71]: call 855-378-4373 or text 55753 – Counselors provide support and education and guide you to the best course of action.

Canada

Alberta[72] (Addiction Helpline, Alberta Health Services)
1-866-332-2322

---

67. https://al-anon.org/newcomers/teen-corner-alateen/

68. https://www.samhsa.gov/find-help/national-helpline

69. https://suicidepreventionlifeline.org/

70. https://www.boystown.org/hotline/Pages/default.aspx

71. https://drugfree.org/article/get-one-on-one-help/

72.   **https://www.albertahealthservices.ca/amh/amh.aspx**

British Columbia[73] (Alcohol and Drug Information and Referral Service)

1-800-663-1441

604-660-9382

Manitoba[74] (Addictions Foundation of Manitoba)

Adult services: 1-855-662-6605

Youth services: 1-877-710-3999

204-944-6200

New Brunswick[75] (Addiction Centres, Department of Health)

506-674-4300

Newfoundland and Labrador[76] (Addictions Services, Department of Health and Community Services)

1-888-737-4668

709-729-3658

Northwest Territories[77] (Department of Health and Social Services)

1-800-661-0844

867-873-7037

Nova Scotia[78] (Mental Health and Addictions Services, Nova Scotia Health Authority)

1-888-429-8167

Nunavut[79] (Kamatsiaqtut Help Line)

1-800-265-3333

867-979-3333

---

73.   http://www.bc211.ca/help-lines/#adirs

74.   http://afm.mb.ca/programs-and-services/

75.   http://www.gnb.ca/0378/centers-e.asp

76.   https://www.health.gov.nl.ca/health/mentalhealth_committee/mentalhealth/ treatment_centres.html

77.   https://www.hss.gov.nt.ca/en/services/addictions/getting-help-addictions

78.   http://www.nshealth.ca/mental-health-addictions

79.   http://www.nunavuthelpline.ca/

Ontario[80] **(ConnexOntario)**

1-866-531-2600

Prince Edward Island[81] **(Addiction Services, Health PEI)**

1-833-553-6983

902-368-4120

Quebec[82] **(Drugs: help and referral)**

1-800-265-2626

514-527-2626

Saskatchewan[83] **(HealthLine, Ministry of Health)**

811 or 1-877-800-0002

306-766-6600

Yukon[84] **(Mental Wellness and Substance Use Services, Health and Social Services)**

1-866-456-3838 (for Yukon, Nunavut and NWT)

867-456-3838

Swiss

+41 31 376 04 01

office@infodrog.ch

Source Reference

https://www.hamburg.com/residents/social/11823820/addiction/

https://alcoholthinkagain.com.au/help/

---

80.   http://www.connexontario.ca/

81.   http://www.healthpei.ca/addictions

82.   http://www.drogue-aidereference.qc.ca/

83.   http://www.saskatchewan.ca/residents/health/accessing-health-care-services/healthline

84.   http://www.hss.gov.yk.ca/mwsu_communities.php

https://www.samsosa.org/wp/help-lines/

https://americanaddictioncenters.org/
rehab-guide/alcohol-drug-hotline

https://www.ccsa.ca/addictions-treatment-
helplines-canada

https://www.infodrog.ch/en/

https://en.m.wikipedia.org/wiki/
National_Suicide_Prevention_Lifeline

https://www.lifeline.org.au[85]

https://www.usa.gov/federal-agencies/
office-on-violence-against-women

https://www.respect.gov.au/services/

https://www.dawncanada.net/issues/
crisis-hotlines/

https://www.admin.ch/gov/en/start/
documentation/
media-releases.msg-id-78545.html

---

85. https://www.lifeline.org.au

https://help.unhcr.org/southafrica/get-help/
violence/

https://www.childhelp.org/contact/

http://worldhelplines.org/canada.html

https://home.crin.org/child-helplines-a-
global-list

Canva

https://www.mayoclinic.org/
healthy-lifestyle/quit-smoking/in-depth/
nicotine-craving/art-20045454

https://www.rauchstopplinie.ch/
index.php/en/

https://drugabuse.com/addiction/
drug-abuse/hotlines/

https://www.blf.org.uk/support-for-you/
smoking/how-can-i-quit

About The Author

Lesiba Ignitiuas Kekana is also known by his stage name Kevin Kekana. He is born in South Africa(Limpopo in a small town called Mokopane). He is born on 25 October 1998. He is also using his pen name (Kevin Rabalao)as a brand to write small project books. In 2019 he wrote 4 books and he decided to take them down from the retailers because he felt like they are not good enough to be in his bookstore. After 3 years then decided to improves his old books and publish them again (one cigarette is one the book he improves). He believes he is the most gifted author that ever walked on earth. His goal is to create the biggest online library with his 2 author brand names. He can write non-friction and friction books. He enjoys most, writing stories and educating others about his discoveries and research. His logo and signature is #IamKevinGotTheMainIdea

.

Copyright